SCALES FOR RATING
THE BEHAVIORAL CHARACTERISTICS
OF SUPERIOR STUDENTS
—
REVISED EDITION

TECHNICAL AND ADMINISTRATION MANUAL

JOSEPH S. RENZULLI

LINDA H. SMITH

ALAN J. WHITE

CAROLYN M. CALLAHAN

ROBERT K. HARTMAN

KAREN L. WESTBERG

Editor
Rachel A. Knox

A sample, *non-reproducible* set of scales is included in this manual.
For additional copies of scales, please contact Creative Learning Press, Inc.
Persons interested in a Spanish language version of the rating scales should contact:
Amaru Ediciones
Malendez, 21,37002 Salamanca, SPAIN
www.verial.es/amaru

Creative Learning Press, Inc.
P.O. Box 320, Mansfield Center, CT 06250
888-518-8004 • www.creativelearningpress.com

Table of Contents

List of Tables

A Personal Note on Identification Systems

Over the years I have responded to numerous questions about identification of the gifted and talented and how the teacher rating scales described in this manual can be used as part of a fail-safe plan for identification. My initial response is always the same: "There is no such thing as a perfect identification system!" Because of situational factors—demographic differences in school populations, various underlying philosophies and beliefs about who is gifted and how best to serve these students, variations in program structures and resources, and differences in state guidelines—each school and district must develop a unique identification system that works best within the contexts and considerations of their school or system. However, I don't want to use this response as a way to dodge the question and fail to deal with the practical need for real people in real schools to develop a plan that is defensible in terms of theory and research and that can be implemented without unusual investments of time, money, or undue paperwork.

The identification system that I have devised and recommended to numerous schools in both the United States and abroad is very specific, and it represents a compromise between the research that led to the development of the Three Ring Conception of Giftedness and the situational factors that vary from school to school. This identification system is included in Appendix F of this manual, and, like most of the work I have done over the years, it can be modified to make it appropriate to local situations. However, in order to maintain the integrity of the rationale and research underlying the system, any and all modifications should respect the basic principles upon which the system is built: that the selection of students for special programs should be based on a relatively equivalent balance of test and non-test based information and that access to enrichment opportunities, resources, and encouragement should not be based on a "one shot" assessment procedure. The concept of "Action Information" (Renzulli, 1986) means that some young people will show their potentials at certain times and under certain circumstances and will therefore need supplementary services at those times. A truly responsive program needs to accommodate such students.

—Joe Renzulli

Renzulli, J. S. (1986). The three-ring conception of giftedness: A developmental model for creative productivity. In Sternberg, R. J., & Davidson, J. (Eds.), *Conceptions of giftedness* (pp. 53-92). New York: Cambridge University Press.

Preface

The *Scales for Rating the Behavioral Characteristics of Superior Students* (*SRBCSS*) was originally published in 1976 by Renzulli, Smith, White, Callahan, and Hartman. The authors developed the instrument to guide teachers or other school personnel in assessing the characteristics of high ability students. Since then, the *Scales for Rating the Behavioral Characteristics of Superior Students* have been used widely throughout the United States (Davis & Rimm, 1994) and have been translated into several languages around the world (e.g., Kalantan, 1991; Srour, 1989; Subhi, 1997).

Over the past twenty years, teachers and researchers have inquired about the potential uses as well as the technical qualities of the rating scales. Some individuals have also offered suggestions for updating *SRBCSS*, including using a different response scale for the items. These inquiries led us to conduct an extensive revision of the scales. Part I of this manual describes the procedures for developing the revised *Scales for Rating the Behavioral Characteristics of Superior Students*, and Part II provides guidelines for administering the scales. (For background information about the development of the original *SRBCSS*, see the technical manual published by Renzulli et al. in 1976.)

PART I: DEVELOPMENT OF THE *SRBCSS-R*

This section explains the judgmental and empirical procedures used to revise the items on the original *Scales for Rating the Behavioral Characteristics of Superior Students* (hereafter referred to as *SRBCSS)* and the methods for conducting two field test administrations of the revised scales. We also present the results from the analyses and the reliability and validity evidence for the revised *Scales for Rating the Behavioral Characteristics of Superior Students* (hereafter referred to as *SRBCSS-R).*

Data-based Literature on Teacher Judgment Instruments

We began the revision process by examining the data-based literature (restricted to articles published after 1976) on teacher judgment instruments developed for rating the characteristics of high-ability students. We examined research reports to determine if we should consider additional behavioral characteristics as well as to learn more about the validity and reliability issues related to teacher judgment instruments in general and, in particular, *SRBCSS.* Teacher judgment instruments have been used for a variety of purposes in research studies by being included with other independent variables such as peer and parent ratings and evaluations of work samples (e.g., Harty, Adkins, & Sherwood, 1984; Singer, Houtz, & Rosenfield, 1992). However, very few teacher judgment instruments have been developed for rating the characteristics of high-ability students, and only a small number of studies have investigated the technical aspects of *SRBCSS.*

A few studies have examined the construct validity or criterion-related validity of teacher judgment instruments for high-ability students. Researchers investigate construct validity to support the instrument developers' assertions that the instruments examine the hypothetical construct(s) being measured. Although techniques for providing construct validity evidence can be quite sophisticated, Popham (1995) emphasizes that there is no single "settles-the-issue-once-and-for-all" investigation (p. 53). Table 1 provides a summary of research studies that have examined the construct validity support for teacher judgment instruments. As indicated, a few researchers have used principal components analysis or confirmatory factor analysis to investigate the underlying constructs of the first four scales of *SRBCSS* (Learning, Creativity, Motivation, and Leadership), which resulted in four or five factor solutions.

Other studies have examined the degree to which teacher ratings predict students' performance on an external criterion—most frequently, a standardized intelligence test. Table 2 presents a summary of the studies in which a teacher judgment instrument was used as a predictor in a criterion-related validity study.

As Table 2 indicates, many instrument developers have used intelligence tests to support the criterion-related validity of their teacher judgment instruments. Several researchers (e.g., Renzulli & Delcourt, 1986) believe that the selection of an intelligence test as a criterion for teacher judgment instruments does not support logical inferences. If teachers' ratings are used to predict performance

Table 1.
Summary of Construct Validity Data on Teacher Judgment Measures

Source	Grade Level	N	Instrument	Procedures	Results	Comments
Burke, Haworth, & Ware (1982)	5-6	368	*SRBCSS:* Learning, Motivation, Creativity, & Leadership	Factor Analysis (PCA)	5 factors emerged; Learning accounted for largest % of variance. 5th factor was labeled "resistance."	Authors suggest breaking up compound items & removing scale headings. Generalizability threatened because high-achieving students comprised sample.
Busse, Dahme, Wagner, & Wierczerkowski (1986)	9-10	Amer., 446 Ger., 434	83-item teacher rating questionnaire	Factor Analysis (PCA)	5 factors for American sample (intelligent, self-centered/neurotic, dynamic/popular, creative, achievement motivated); 7 factors for German sample.	Authors believed results conform quite well to Renzulli's scales. Artistically & academically gifted were in the sample. American factors accounted for 45.6% of the variance.
Gridley (1984)	3-4	152	*SRBCSS:* Learning, Motivation, Creativity, & Leadership	Confirmatory Factor Analysis (LISREL)	4 factor solution; the 4th was labeled "nonconformity." High correlation among the factors (.55-.87).	Explanations: 4 constructs underlie first 3 scales, items are related to more than 1 construct, or labeling of scales cause "response set."
Lowrance & Anderson (1977)	1-5	192	*SRBCSS:* Learning, Motivation, Creativity, & Leadership	Factor Analysis (PCA)	2 factors emerged, accounting for 87.6% of the variance.	Statistical tables for PCA weren't shown.
Perrone & Chen (1982)	11-12	67	Male/Perrone GIFTS instrument	Cluster Analysis (CLUSTAN)— teacher, parents, & students completed the scales.	6 clusters: divergent, goal orientation, task persistency, intraceptive, social awareness, & social effectiveness.	Authors believe this instrument should be used to supplement traditional identification measures & to identify areas for affective programming. FA would provide more information.

on intelligence tests, what is the rationale for using teachers' ratings? Why second guess intelligence tests? Experts assert that performance in a gifted education program or academic success is a better criterion for supporting the criterion-related validity of a teacher judgment instrument (Feldhusen, Asher, & Hoover, 1984; Renzulli & Delcourt, 1986).

Table 2.

Summary of Criterion-Related Validity Data on Teacher Judgment Measures

Source	Grade Level	N	Judgment Measure	Criterion Measure	Procedures	Results	Comments
Argulewicz, Elliot, & Hall (1982)	1-6	525	*SRBCSS*: Learning, Motivation, Creativity, & Leadership	Minimum P97 on intelligence test & P96 on achievement test	Comparisons of differences (MANOVA) in ratings of Anglo-Amer. & Mex.-Amer. gifted children.	Significant differences between groups on Learning & Motivation ratings (p<.05).	Possible explanations: Mex.-Amer. children exhibit fewer learning & motivation behavior, ethnic bias of raters, or *SRBCSS* lacks validity for culturally different.
Ashman & Vukelich (1983)	K-5	183	*SRBCSS* & 3 forms of a 26-item behavioral rating scale (A, B, C)	125 + Otis Lennon	11 teachers completed all 4 instruments (random order). Effectiveness and efficiency were compared. Multiple R with 4 forms & Otis Lennon.	*SRBCSS* was most effective, but time-consuming. Small amount of variation on Otis was accounted for by 4 forms. No regression tables.	Authors recommend Form C, which is similar to *SRBCSS*. IQ criterion problem.
Borland (1978)	3-6	195	Teacher rating scale in Middletown, NJ	CTMM & ITBS	Pearson correlation & multiple correlation of 2 ratings w/ CTMM & ITBS.	Significant, moderate, positive correlations.	Study supported the use of ratings. Regression tables weren't shown.
Cummings (1980)	K-6	204	31-item Cummings Checklist of Characteristics (CC)	WISC-R or Stanford-Binet & CA MGM criteria for identifying gifted.	Examined how CC discriminated (Chi-square & DFA) between (1) gifted & non-gifted (2) test identified gifted (TIG) & non-test identified gifted (NTIG).	8 CC items discriminated gifted & non-gifted. No items discriminated TIG & NTIG.	No validity or reliability information reported for the CC. Tables w/ statistical results and probability levels were not provided.
Elliot, Argulewicz, & Turco (1986)	3-6	402	*SRBCSS*: Learning, Motivation, Creativity, & Planning	Stanford Achievement Test, WISC-R or Stanford-Binet	Regression analysis for 3 groups: Anglo, mid/high SES; Anglo, low SES; & Hispanic, low SES (all of whom were in gifted programs).	In general, Hispanic ratings accounted for greatest variation in SAT Reading & Anglo, mid/high SES ratings accounted for greatest variation in SAT Math. Minimum correlation between IQ & *SRBCSS*.	Homogeneity of subjects' achievement limits generalizability. *SRBCSS* may have value for identifying gifted Hispanic students.
Glassnapp, Kros, Issac, Hitz, & Carlton (1981)	K-5	68	32-item teacher rating instrument	Groups: gifted (WISC-R> 125) & non-gifted	Factor analysis was done on the instrument & was used with non-verbal tasks to predict group membership (DFA).	Teacher ratings alone weren't significant. When combined w/ non-verbal tasks, 89% of gifted and 84% of the non-gifted (p<.05) were correctly classified.	IQ criterion & small *N*: p ratio limits meaningfulness. No literature support for items.

Table 2 (cont.).

Summary of Criterion-Related Validity Data on Teacher Judgment Measures

Source	Grade Level	N	Judgment Measure	Criterion Measure	Procedures	Results	Comments
Hunter & Lowe (1978)	4-5	34	*SRBCSS*: Learning, Motivation, Creativity, & Leadership	120+ WISC-R	Regression analysis included. Otis & ITBS w/*SRBCSS* to predict WISC-R.	Multiple R=.65. Variance at each step was not reported.	Small sample size is a limitation. IQ criterion problem.
Karnes, Chauvin, & Trant (1984)	9-12	199	H. S. Personality Questionnaire: Leadership Potential Scores	Groups: Elected leaders & non-elected students in g/t high school.	DFA	Small variance (6.6%) in groups was accounted for by factor 1: tenderminded, sensitive, & overprotected.	Meaningfulness is limited because students were homogeneous in achievement.
Kysilka, Ferguson, Wiles, Johene, & Jean (1979)	Elem.	126	Annehurst Curriculum Classification System (ACCS): 6 categories	*SRBCSS*: Learning, Motivation, Creativity, & Leadership	6 categories of ACCS were paired and correlated w/ the 4 *SRBCSS*.	Pearson correlations were moderate & significant (p<.05).	Weakness in sampling & data collection. Multiple regression would make results more meaningful.
Lowrance & Anderson (1977)	1-5	192	*SRBCSS*: Learning, Motivation, Creativity, & Leadership. WISC-R: 10 subscales	Groups: gifted & non-gifted place-ment ("university decision")	DFA	WISC-R subscales & first 3 *SRBCSS* were significant predictors of group membership.	Criteria for gifted placement wasn't defined or explained. Perhaps predictors and criterion were the same?
Mayfield (1979)	3	573, 94% Mex.-Amer.	Teacher ratings and rankings (Q-Sort) of intelligence, achievement, & creativity	TTCT, CTBS, & CAT	Pearson correlation of teacher ratings & rankings w/ criterion measures.	Most correlations significant, but coefficients were not provided. Correlation of creativity ratings & rankings w/ TICT were not significant.	Multiple regression should have been used. Teacher ratings were of overall intelligence, achievement, & creativity.
Rust & Lose (1980)	1-7	109	*SRBCSS*: Learning, Motivation, Creativity, & Leadership	130+ WISC-R	Regression included 10 predictors; Slosson & *SRBCSS* were primary ones.	*SRBCSS* did not significantly add to the equation.	Complete statistical tables aren't shown. IQ criterion problem.
Swenson (1978)	4-6	90	Teacher generated checklist of creative behavior for disadvantaged	Stanford Achievement Test & TTCT	Correlation	r=.39 w/SAT (p<.001) r=.08w/TTCT (ns)	Content validity concern (i.e., experts would not agree that items assess creativity).

4

The literature on data-based investigations of teacher judgment instruments and conclusions about the "continued relevancy" of *SRBCSS* (e.g., Friedman, & Murphy, 1992) support the continued use of *SRBCSS* to assess the characteristics of high-ability students. As a result of these findings, we piloted a revised version of the first four scales of *SRBCSS* (Learning, Creativity, Motivation, and Leadership) with a large sample of teachers across the country to provide evidence of the validity and reliability of the revised instrument.

Development of the Revised Scales

We made four types of modifications to the original *SRBCSS* items. First, we eliminated compound items from the original scales. For example, one of the original Learning items was, "Has unusually advanced vocabulary for age or grade level; uses terms in a meaningful way; has verbal behavior characterized by richness of expression, elaboration, and fluency." We changed this item to "demonstrates advanced vocabulary for age or grade level." Second, we reworded the items to include gender neutral pronouns. Third, we added new items to reflect characteristics of high-ability students that are supported in other research studies on teacher judgment instruments. For example, we added "the ability to concentrate intently for a long period of time" as a Motivation item on the field test edition because of the empirical support obtained by Glassnapp, Kros, Isaac, Hitz, & Carlton (1981) for the characteristic. Fourth, we reworded the original items slightly to make the syntax agree with a statement listed as the beginning phrase for all item stems: "The student demonstrates . . ." After making these four modifications, we listed 56 potential items for the first field test of the instrument.

In addition to making item modifications, we changed the response format on the revised instrument. Some teachers and specialists expressed dissatisfaction with the 4-point response scale on the original scales (1 = seldom/never, 2 = occasionally, 3 = considerably, and 4 = almost always) because they did not perceive the four points as being on an interval scale. For example, they did not view the distance between "seldom/never" and "occasionally" as equal to the distance between "occasionally" and "considerably." Therefore, we employed a 6-point response scale on the revised instrument: 1 = never, 2 = very rarely, 3 = rarely, 4 = occasionally, 5 = frequently, 6 = always.

Content Validity Support

Content validity evidence refers to the extent to which items adequately sample from the intended domain of content (Cronbach, 1971). While the content validation process began with a review of the literature, we developed the *Experts' Rating Form for Teacher Judgment of Behavioral Characteristics of Superior Students* (see Table 3) to provide the primary support for the instrument's content validity. We sent the *Experts' Rating Form* to 60 experts in gifted education who examined the relationship between the operational and conceptual definitions of the 56 items. The experts selected the category to which each item corresponded (Cognition, Creativity, Motivation, Leadership) and indicated how strongly they felt each item matched the category (1= very certain,

2 = fairly certain, and 3 = not very certain). If the experts thought a characteristic did not match any of the categories, they explained their reasoning. Fifty-three of the 60 experts returned the rating forms, and 51 returned a postcard indicating their willingness to be included on a published list of experts who provided the ratings (see back cover of manual or page iii).

Table 3 displays a summary of the experts' ratings for the 56 items, including the percentage of experts who selected each category for each item (with the a priori category underlined) as well as the mean strength ratings. Criteria for maintaining items on the first field test were as follows: (1) agreement by 70% or more of the experts about the categorization of items and (2) mean strength ratings at or above 1.75.

As shown on Table 3, 15 items did not meet the > 70% agreement on any one factor or minimum 1.75 mean strength criteria, and we dropped these items from the instrument. More than 70% of the experts placed four items (Items 2, 22, 23, and 39) in categories that were not the a priori categories, and we included these items on the first field test version of the instrument. We added 16 new items to the remaining 41 items and sent a modified version of the *Expert's Rating Form* to 11 of the original 60 experts for additional ratings. As before, experts selected the conceptual definitions to which they believed each item corresponded and indicated how certain they felt about their placement of each item. After examining the results from these ratings, we added 13 of these new items, making a total of 54 items on the version of the instrument sent to teachers throughout the country for the first field test.

First Field Test Procedures and Results

In the first field test, educators who hold graduate degrees and have direct experience in gifted education programs asked K-12 teachers in their school districts to complete ratings using the 54 items. We used a systematic, random sampling procedure to select students for the ratings. Teachers rated just four students in their classes: the third and eighth boy and the third and eighth girl as determined by their class rosters (an alphabetical list by last name). By selecting students in this manner, we anticipated there would be greater variability in responses, an important consideration for principal components analyses. In addition to completing the ratings, teachers indicated each student's general academic achievement level on a 5-point scale (1 = high, 2 = high average, 3 = average, 4 = low average, and 5 = low).

For this field test, teachers completed ratings on 921 students in Grades K-12, the majority of whom were Grade 3-6 students ($n = 513$). On the ratings of general academic achievement level, teachers rated 239 students as high, 262 as high average, 238 as average, 108 as low average, and 70 as low. Achievement levels were missing from four of the ratings.

We performed principal components analysis on the *SRBCSS-R* ratings from the first field test, which resulted in a four factor solution that accounted for 72% of the variance. Because 46 items had loadings of .40 or higher on the first factor (rather than being distributed among a few factors), we considered the results unsatisfactory. We hypothesized three reasons for this result. First, despite the

Table 3.
Summary of Ratings on the *Experts' Rating Form for Teacher Judgement of Behavioral Characteristics of Superior Students*

Categories	Conceptual Definitions
I Cognition	Behaviors that reflect an individual's ability to perceive and acquire knowledge.
II Creativity	Behaviors that reflect an individual's ability to produce original, novel, and unique ideas or products.
III Motivation	Behaviors that reflect an individual's ability to bring energy to bear on problems or tasks.
IV Leadership	Behaviors that reflect an individual's ability to guide or direct actions by other individuals.
V None of the Above	

Items	Percentage of Experts Selecting Each Category (A Priori category is underlined)					Mean Strength Ratings (3-point scale)
	I	II	III	IV	V	
The student demonstrates . . .						
1. intellectual curiosity about many topics.	67	19	<u>14</u>	0	0	1.49
2. responsible behavior; can be counted on to follow through on activities/projects.	0	0	72	<u>21</u>	4	1.50
3. the ability to concentrate intently on a topic for a long period of time.	13	0	<u>81</u>	0	6	1.43
4. stubbornness in beliefs.	4	23	<u>23</u>	9	42	1.81
5. imaginative thinking ability.	2	<u>96</u>	0	0	2	1.25
6. advanced vocabulary for his or her age or grade level.	<u>96</u>	2	0	0	2	1.26
7. persistence when pursuing goals.	2	0	<u>96</u>	2	0	1.23
8. the ability to make generalizations about events, people, and things.	<u>87</u>	6	0	6	0	1.26
9. a willingness to accept disorder.	2	<u>79</u>	2	2	15	1.37
10. pleasure in being around others; sociability.	0	0	2	<u>87</u>	11	1.74
11. a large storehouse of information about a specific topic.	<u>96</u>	2	0	0	2	1.14
12. a keen sense of humor.	9	<u>72</u>	6	4	11	1.63
13. interest in independent reading.	<u>67</u>	2	17	0	8	1.52
14. a tendency to be well-liked by classmates.	0	0	0	<u>90</u>	10	1.46
15. the ability to articulate ideas and communicate well with others.	21	0	0	<u>74</u>	6	1.49
16. recall of factual information.	<u>98</u>	0	0	0	2	1.15
17. sensitivity to beauty and the aesthetic characteristics of things.	0	<u>91</u>	2	0	8	1.32
18. persistent work on tasks even when setbacks occur.	2	4	<u>94</u>	0	0	1.02
19. emotional sensitivity.	0	<u>60</u>	0	18	22	1.88
20. an adventurous spirit or a willingness to take risks.	0	<u>85</u>	6	2	8	1.42
21. self-confidence when interacting with age peers.	0	2	0	<u>89</u>	8	1.32
22. verbal behavior characterized by "richness" of expression, elaboration, and fluency.	<u>22</u>	71	0	0	4	1.42
23. interest in many "adult" topics, such as religion, politics, race, and ethics.	79	0	<u>9</u>	6	6	1.36

Table 3 (cont.).

24. insight into cause and effect relationships.	87	8	2	2	2	1.25
25. uninhibited expressions of opinion.	4	62	0	8	27	1.76
26. the ability to define the final goal or outcome of an activity or project.	13	8	26	43	9	1.75
27. a tendency to direct an activity when he or she is involved with others.	2	4	4	89	2	1.23
28. boredom with routine tasks.	15	62	13	0	9	1.77
29. a tendency to see humor in situations that may not appear to be humorous to others.	8	79	2	2	9	1.64
30. perfectionistic behavior.	15	0	32	0	45	1.80
31. keen and insightful observations.	76	24	0	0	0	1.43
32. provocative questioning behavior (as distinct from informational or factual questioning).	25	68	0	0	8	1.49
33. a large storehouse of information about a variety of topics.	96	2	0	0	2	1.15
34. cooperative behavior when working with teachers or students.	0	0	2	71	27	1.60
35. intense involvement in certain topics or problems.	10	12	72	2	4	1.30
36. the ability to generate a large number of ideas or solutions to problems or questions.	6	82	8	0	0	1.17
37. the ability to deal with abstractions.	83	17	0	0	0	1.16
38. the ability to grasp underlying principles.	96	4	0	0	0	1.09
39. a preference for non-fiction reading materials (biographies, autobiographies, reference books . . .).	71	2	8	8	19	1.53
40. the ability to come up with unusual, unique, or clever responses.	6	94	0	0	0	1.17
41. a concern with adapting, improving, or modifying objects, ideas, institutions, or systems.	9	74	6	9	0	1.06
42. a resistance to sex-role stereotyping.	2	53	4	8	33	1.68
43. the ability to generate responses that fall into different categories.	8	92	0	0	0	1.30
44. behavior that requires little direction from teachers.	4	4	79	4	10	1.41
45. effort toward understanding complicated material through analytical reasoning ability.	87	0	11	0	2	1.32
46. participation in a variety of extra- or co-curricular activities.	2	0	19	48	31	1.63
47. the ability to state and define goals and priorities of others even when they are not the same as his or her own.	6	0	2	85	8	1.42
48. little need for external motivation to follow through in work that is initially exciting.	0	0	98	2	0	1.26
49. assertive (perhaps even aggressive) behavior.	0	4	8	44	44	1.85
50. behavior for organizing and bringing structure to things, people, and situations.	10	6	4	80	0	1.42
51. an unwillingness to accept authoritarian pronouncements without critical examination.	23	40	2	15	19	1.80
52. intellectual playfulness, willingness to fantasize, and manipulate ideas.	4	92	2	0	2	1.19
53. a non-conforming attitude, does not fear being different.	0	85	2	2	11	1.25
54. the ability to transfer learning from one situation to another.	75	24	2	0	0	1.31
55. behavior directed at discovering the why and how of things.	61	25	12	0	0	1.44
56. preference for independent work.	6	25	54	0	15	1.66

Note: Some items had missing data, and percentages on categories may not total 100% due to rounding.

8

random selection of students on the student rosters, teachers rated the majority of the students, for whatever reason, as "high average" and "high" in general achievement, which explains the low (<.6) standard deviations on the items. Second, the sample included students living in similar socio-economic circumstances; for example, 64% of the students lived in medium-sized, middle-class communities, and 94% were Caucasian. Third, the majority of the students were enrolled in Grades 3-6, and we found grade level differences when examining the factor structure. Therefore, we concluded that the 13-year age span in the student sample was too large. Because of concerns about sampling bias and unacceptable evidence for the construct validity, we revised some items as well as the sampling procedures for a second field test.

Second Field Test Procedures

After examining the loadings from the principal components analyses from the first field test, we deleted some Learning items and added some Motivation items to the instrument. As a result, we created a 43-item instrument (i. e., 13 Learning, 11 Creativity, 11 Motivation, and 8 Leadership items) for the second field test. (We later removed five of these items, as described in the construct validity section that follows.) In addition to making modifications to the items, we made a few procedural changes. Since the original *SRBCSS* was published, some individuals have inquired about the degree to which response bias may impact the ratings on the scales because the headings (Learning, Creativity, Motivation, and Leadership) are listed above the respective items. To address this issue, we used two formats of the revised scales in the second field test. The first format included the headings (Learning, Creativity, Motivation, and Leadership) above the respective items, and the second format included the items interspersed throughout the instrument with no headings. The subsequent principal component analyses of the two data sets indicated that the "variance accounted for" on the two versions was very similar. Although the initial factor structure was slightly better (i. e., the items loaded a bit more closely with the a priori factors on the format without the headings), the overall validity and reliability support was somewhat stronger for the version that included the headings. Therefore, we selected the second format (found in Appendix A) for *SRBCSS-R* and report the analyses for this format hereafter.

Sampling Procedure

Educators with extensive experience in regular and gifted education and persons holding graduate degrees in gifted education participated in the second field test by serving as local liaisons. These educators ($N = 19$) were employed as gifted education specialists or administrators in the following states and province: Alabama, California, Florida, Louisiana, Massachusetts, Michigan, New Hampshire, New York, Ontario, Pennsylvania, South Carolina, and Washington. In the fall, the liaisons asked teachers (146 male, 426 female) of students in Grades 3-12 to rate the above-average students in their classrooms using *SRBCSS-R* as well as to provide demographic information about students. Liaisons instructed teachers to complete the ratings on "above-average students," defined as (a) students who perform above the 70th percentile on a standardized achievement test (composite score), (b) students who perform above the 70th percentile on a majority of their standardized achievement subtests, or (c) students who receive primarily A and B school-assigned grades in academic subjects. In addition, liaisons encouraged teachers to provide ratings of students who they perceived to be above-average in ability, but who didn't match one of the aforementioned categories.

As a result of these instructions, the version of the scales with the headings was completed on 572 students (i. e., 268 boys and 303 girls [gender was missing on one form]). There were no significant differences in the total score *SRBCSS-R* ratings between boys and girls (t = -.177, df = 568, $p > .05$). The scales were completed on students in Grades 3 through 12: $n = 67, 105, 106, 51, 39, 59, 53, 24, 57, 10$, respectively (grade level was missing on one form). An analysis of variance indicated differences among grade levels (F [9,5600] = 5.212, $p < .01$), but the Scheffé post hoc analysis revealed that the difference occurred only between the ratings of 10th graders and four other grade levels. Only 3 teachers completed the ratings of the 10th graders, and the ratings were significantly higher than the mean ratings of the other grade levels. Because there were no significant differences when compared with each other ($p > .05$), the ratings of the 10th graders appear to be an anomaly. Although the majority of the sample was Caucasian, it represented the ethnic makeup of the general population. Of the 562 student ratings, 309 were completed on students who had been identified for their local gifted education programs.

We had additional instruments completed on two subsamples. To provide interrater reliability estimates of the instrument, the first subsample was a group of junior high students ($n = 65$) who each received ratings by two teachers. The second subsample was comprised of students in Grades 3-12 ($n = 87$) on whom gifted education specialists completed an instrument entitled *Rating Student Performance in a Gifted Program (RSP/GP)* (Appendix B) to provide evidence of the criterion-related validity of the *SRBCSS-R*.

Construct Validity Support

We performed exploratory principal components analysis to examine the relationships between the judgmentally developed categories and empirically derived constructs. When testing hypotheses about the interrelationships among items, Gable and Wolf (1993) explained that

> derived constructs are examined in light of the theoretical predictions that follow from the literature review and operational definition of the target categories specified during the content validity process. Thus, we can, in one sense, consider any factor analysis executed for the purpose of supporting factor analysis to be of a confirmatory nature. (p. 106)

We conducted principal components analysis using SPSS-X (SPSS, 1988). Using Kaiser's criterion for estimating eigenvalues (i. e., greater than 1.0), four factors were extracted. After examining the factor loadings, we removed five items to improve the factor structure (Items 5, 12, 17, 22, and 43). This revision resulted in a four-factor solution that accounted for 71% of the variance—

namely, four factors that included 38 items: 11 learning, 9 creativity, 11 motivation, and 7 leadership. Varimax and oblique rotations yielded a similar factor structure and similar item loadings. Table 4 shows the factor pattern matrix with the oblique rotation.

The 38 items that loaded on the four factors made conceptual sense, and we named the factors

Table 4.
SRBCSS-R Factor Loading Matrix With Oblique Rotation (N = 572)

Item Stems	I	II	III	IV
Factor I: Learning				
7. an understanding of complicated material through analytical reasoning ability.	.89			
4. the ability to grasp underlying principles.	.87			
9. the ability to deal with abstractions.	.86			
6. insight into cause and effect relationships.	.84			
2. the ability to make generalizations about events, people, and things.	.82			
11. keen and insightful observations.	.79			
1. advanced vocabulary for his or her age or grade level.	.77			
8. a large storehouse of information about a variety of topics.	.68			
3. large storehouse of information about a specific topic.	.65			
13. the ability to transfer learnings from one situation to another.	.65			
10. recall of factual information.	.65			
Factor II: Creativity				
14. imaginative thinking ability.	.48	.48		
19. the ability to generate a large number of ideas or solutions to problems or questions.	.42	.39		
20. a tendency to see humor in situations that may not appear to be humorous to others.		.80		
23. intellectual playfulness, willingness to fantasize and manipulate ideas.		.77		
24. a non-conforming attitude, does not fear being different.		.77		
18. an adventurous spirit or a willingness to take risks.		.73		
15. a sense of humor.		.70		
16. the ability to come up with unusual, unique, or clever responses.	.31	.66		
21. the ability to adapt, improve, or modify objects or ideas.	.36	.38		
Factor III: Leadership				
37. a tendency to be respected by classmates.			.87	
39. self-confidence when interacting with age peers.			.33	.76
41. cooperative behavior when working with others.			.76	
40. the ability to organize and bring structure to things, people, and situations.			.69	
38. the ability to articulate ideas and communicate well with others.			.63	
42. a tendency to direct an activity when he or she is involved with others.			.31	.61
36. responsible behavior, can be counted on to follow through on activities/projects.			.45	.57
Factor IV. Motivation				
33. commitment to long term projects when interested in a topic.				.90
32. intense involvement in certain topics or problems.				.89
31. follow-through behavior when interested in a topic or problem.				.88
34. persistence when pursuing goals.				.87
27. sustained interest in certain topics or problems.				.81
29. persistent work on tasks even when setbacks occur.				.79
28. tenacity for finding out information on topics of interest.				.79
35. little need for external motivation to follow through in work that is initially exciting.				.79
25. the ability to concentrate intently on a topic for a long period of time.				.76
30. a preference for situations in which he or she can take personal responsibility for the outcomes of his or her efforts.				.72
26. behavior that requires little direction from teachers.				.35	.63

Note: Only loadings above .30 have been included in this table.

"Learning," "Creativity," "Motivation," and "Leadership." The items defining the Learning factor described the degree to which students exhibited various learning behaviors. A student with a high rating on this factor would exhibit the ability to grasp underlying principles, deal with abstractions, etc. Likewise, the items defining the Creativity factor described the degree to which students exhibited various creativity characteristics. A student with a high rating on this factor would exhibit characteristics such as the ability to generate a large number of ideas (fluent thinking), the ability to generate unique ideas (original thinking), and a willingness to fantasize and manipulate ideas. As indicated in Table 4, the item composition of the empirically extracted factors was nearly the same as the item composition of the four a priori factors. We found minor differences on three items. Items 14 and 19 loaded on both Factor 1 (Learning) and Factor 2 (Creativity). Item 36 loaded most strongly on Factor 4 (Motivation), but loaded almost as strongly on Factor 3 (Leadership), which was judgmentally perceived to be a Leadership item. In summary, the derived factors were nearly identical to the judgmental factors, providing strong support for the construct validity of the scales. Table 5 presents the factor intercorrelation matrix. As these correlations indicate, the factors were relatively distinct. Appendix C includes a sample of the final *SRBCSS-R* instrument.

Alpha Reliability

We computed Cronbach's alpha reliability estimates for the four scales derived from the principal components analysis described above. The alpha reliability coefficients for the Learning, Creativity, Motivation, and Leadership factors were r =.91, r =.84, r =. 90, r =.87, respectively. The alpha reliability for the instrument as a whole was r = .97. These coefficients provide strong support for the internal consistency of the instrument.

Criterion-related Evidence of Validity

As stated earlier, gifted education specialists in some districts completed the *Rating Student Performance in a Gifted Program* instrument (Renzulli & Westberg, 1991) to provide predictive validity support of *SRBCSS-R*. The instrument (see Appendix B) contains 10 items, such as "This year, [the student] created quality projects." Using a 5-point response scale that ranged from "very low degree" to "very high degree," teachers indicated the degree to which they observed the behavior in a particular student. On the original field test of the *RSP/GP* instrument, gifted education

Table 5.
Factor Intercorrelation Matrix from the Oblique Rotation (*N* = 572)

	Factor I	Factor II	Factor III	Factor IV
Factor I: Learning	1.00			
Factor II: Creativity	.46	1.00		
Factor III: Leadership	.26	.25	1.00	
Factor IV: Motivation	-.55	-.25	-.48	1.00

specialists in three states rated the performance of 433 students in Grades 1-9 who had been participating in a gifted education program for several months. Principal components analysis on these data revealed a one factor solution (which was anticipated and desired) that accounted for 68.8% of the variance, and the alpha reliability coefficient was r = .95.

For the *SRBCSS-R* field test study, gifted education specialists completed the *RSP/GP* instrument in the spring on a subsample of students ($n = 87$) whose classroom teachers had completed *SRBCSS-R* ratings for them in the fall (i. e., gifted education specialists rated students after they had been participating in a local gifted education program for several months). We conducted principal components analysis on the *RSP/GP* data, and one factor was again extracted. The alpha reliability of the instrument when completed by the gifted education specialists described above was r = .94, providing strong evidence of its internal consistency.

We found that the Pearson correlation between the *SRBCSS-R* and the *Rating Student Performance in a Gifted Program* ratings was r = .40, a moderate correlation. In addition to calculating a correlation, we conducted a stepwise regression analysis using both the *Rating Student Performance in a Gifted Program* total scores and standardized achievement test composite scores as independent variables and the *SRBCSS-R* ratings as the dependent variable. The tolerance level for each variable entry step was set at $p < .01$. The regression results indicated that the *SRBCSS-R* ratings entered at step 1 and yielded a multiple R of .42, $p < .001$, explaining 17.6% of the variance. The achievement test composite scores did not enter the equation and, accordingly, did not significantly increase the multiple correlation. Hence, the *SRBCSS-R* ratings were a significant predictor of success in a gifted program as measured by the *Rating Student Performance in a Gifted Program*.

Interrater Reliability

We performed two procedures to obtain estimates of the interrater reliability of the *SRBCSS-R*. As stated earlier, two teachers in different subject areas (such as a mathematics teacher and a language arts teacher or a social studies teacher and a language arts teacher) completed ratings on a small subsample of middle school or junior high students ($n = 65$). The majority of the students received ratings by a mathematics teacher and a language arts teacher. First, we obtained a Pearson correlation coefficient of r = .50 ($p < .01$) between the mean total instrument ratings made by the two teachers. While this correlation is moderate, it is quite respectable when considering that teachers of different subject areas observe different behaviors in students. In addition to calculating the correlation between the two ratings, we computed the intraclass correlation coefficient between the two ratings (r = .65). Again, this coefficient is moderate, but fairly respectable given the fact that teachers of different subjects, such as a mathematics teacher and a language teacher, would observe at least some different characteristics in students.

14

PART II: ADMINISTRATION OF THE *SRBCSS-R*

This section provides instructions for administering and interpreting the *Scales for Rating the Behavioral Characteristics of Superior Students-R* (*SRBCSS-R*) and describes purposes for using the scales, guidelines for using the scales correctly, a teacher training exercise, and how to establish local norms. School districts have often misused the original scales, and we want to be clear about their appropriate use. To improve the validity of the interpretations from the scales, it is important that those administering the scales adhere to certain procedures.

Purposes for Using the Scales

The *Scales for Rating the Behavioral Characteristics of Superior Students-R (SRBCSS-R)* can be used for a variety of purposes. While identifying students is the most frequent use, educators can administer the scales to assess student strengths and include the results in documents such as the *Total Talent Portfolio* (Purcell & Renzulli, 1998). The scales can also be used for research purposes, such as assessing the effects of various interventions. The primary purpose for the scales, however, is to screen and select students who will receive gifted education services. Because regulations vary from state to state, identification plans differ widely throughout the country. Nonetheless, most districts request some form of teacher input, and the *SRBCSS-R* provides a source of non-test information.

A guiding principle in programming for gifted and talented students is that identification procedures should bear a direct relationship to the types of educational experiences for which students are being selected. For this reason, instrument administrators should select only those scales that are relevant to program objectives. School staffs will waste a great deal of time and effort if they do not give careful consideration to which scales will yield the most appropriate information when selecting participants for a particular program. Asking teachers to complete all of the scales for a group of students is a burdensome task and could result in superficial or hastily completed ratings. Generally, the first three or four scales (the ones that have been revised) are consistent with the objectives of most gifted education programs and services. Educators should consider the behaviors in the other seven scales only as they relate to the goals and objectives of a particular program.

Guidelines for Using the Scales

Guideline No. 1: Consider the type of program for which students are being identified. School districts that provide program services for developing students' learning and creativity behaviors, for example, may consider using the Learning and Creativity scales. For a program that provides accelerated mathematical instruction only, it may be inappropriate to have teachers complete the creativity scale. In particular, schools that use the Three-Ring Conception of Giftedness as an underlying philosophy for their enrichment programs should consider having teachers rate students' behaviors using *SRBCSS-R*. An explanation of a complete identification system is beyond the scope of this manual, and readers should review identification procedures in other publications, such as the *Schoolwide Enrichment Model* (Renzulli & Reis, 1997) and "A Practical System for Identifying Gifted and Talented Students" (Renzulli, 1990).

Guideline No. 2: Examine each scale separately. **Do not add the scores from the various scales together to form a total score!** Because the dimensions (scales) of the *SRBCSS-R* represent relatively different sets of behavioral characteristics, users must separately analyze students' ratings on each of the respective scales. By forming a composite or total score, students' unique strengths are overlooked. The scales provide teachers and administrators with the opportunity to focus on specific student strengths, and school staff should develop learning experiences that take into account the area or areas in which a student has received high ratings. For example, a student who receives high ratings on the Motivation scale will probably profit most from a program that emphasizes self-initiated pursuits and an independent study approach to learning. A student with high ratings on the Leadership scale should be given opportunities to organize activities.

In addition to looking at a student's profile of scores on individual scales for identification purposes, teachers can gather additional insight into student abilities and characteristics by analyzing student ratings on individual scale items. These items call attention to differences in behavioral characteristics and in most cases suggest the kinds of educational experiences that are most likely to represent the students preferred method or style of learning. Thus, a careful analysis of scale items can assist teachers in their efforts to develop individualized programs for students.

Guideline No. 3: **Do not modify or abbreviate the scales by reducing the number of items on each scale!** When some items on a scale are modified or eliminated, the reliability estimates of the scales are lower. For example, if only three items on the leadership scale had been used in the field study (Items 1, 3, 5), the alpha reliability estimate would decrease from $r = .87$ to $r = .62$. Reducing the number of items is like taking a shortcut on an automobile trip and ending up at the wrong place!

Teacher Training Exercise

To improve the reliability of teacher ratings and to help classroom teachers understand the key concepts and specific behaviors represented in the first four scales of *SRBCSS-R*, we recommend that teachers and administrators complete the Teacher Training Exercise for the *SRBCSS-R* (located in Appendix D), which was designed and field tested to facilitate discussions about specific student behaviors.

First, if participants are not familiar with *SRBCSS-R*, provide them with copies of the actual scales and indicate that the training activity is different from the actual rating process. Ask participants to engage in the first task, which consists of matching key concepts with the *SRBCSS-R* scale items. Teachers may do one scale at a time or do all four scales at one time. Ask the total group to compare their responses to the suggested answer key and discuss some of the variations in their responses. Be certain to point out that there are usually some variations in opinion about responses as there is no one correct answer for each item. Call attention to the items about which there is disagreement among participants and suggest that these items be given special consideration for the second task that they are to complete in small groups.

For the second task, divide participants into small groups of approximately 5 to 10 persons. Working individually, each participant should list the behaviors of students they believe are good exemplars of the scale items. Encourage participants to recall actual behaviors and students with whom they have worked, rather than hypothetical examples. Participants in each group should then discuss their examples with each other and attempt to reach consensus on one or two examples that they believe are the *best* representations of each scale item. The entire group should then come back together and each subgroup should present their best examples to the total group. Encourage discussion and comparison among subgroups and, once again, emphasize the legitimacy of variations in opinion.

Interpreting the Results

After classroom teachers have completed the *SRBCSS*-R ratings, either the teachers or a third party should compute and record the total points for each scale. If schools are using the scales to identify and consider students for special services and programs, they should develop local norms (i.e., scores such as percentile ranks, which indicate how each student compares relative to his or her peers). **We do not offer national norms for *SRBCSS-R* because we do not believe that this information is meaningful or appropriate.** Populations differ from school district to school district, and even between and among schools in the same district. Similarly, developmental differences exist between grade levels, and, therefore, even local norms should be calculated for individual grade levels. Unlike normed instruments such as standardized tests, which compare students across the entire population, *SRBCSS-R* is purposefully designed to access student strategies within a local reference group. Furthermore, regardless of the demographic characteristics of a school district, the students who receive the highest ratings on the scales are the students who need services above and beyond the curriculum provided for a majority of the students within each setting. **The importance of calculating *local* norms cannot be overemphasized!**

The step-by-step procedure for calculating local norms—percentile ranks—is outlined in Appendix E. A percentile rank indicates the ranking of one student relative to other students in the comparison group. For example, a person whose rating was equivalent to a percentile rank of 85 means that the individual was rated higher than or, as well as, 85% of the other individuals who received ratings on that scale within that particular setting. This procedure should be completed for each scale. As an alternative to calculating each student's local percentile rank with pencil and paper, the ratings and a formula can be entered on a computer spreadsheet program, such as Microsoft® Excel, for quicker calculations.

Final Note

Most would agree that obtaining teacher input is extremely valuable when selecting students who will receive special services or participate in gifted education programs. The *SRBCSS-R* allows this information to be gathered in a more structured and standardized manner. As with test score information, however, weighted scores from the scales are not perfectly reliable; they represent an attempt to obtain more objective information about student behaviors. The ratings do not provide the complete and final snapshot of a student's characteristics. For that reason, as with test score information, a *SRBCSS-R* rating should not be the single criterion for selecting students for special programs. The information should be used in conjunction with other information. Schools should also keep in mind that identification of students for gifted programs is not the most important task; rather the truly important task is to formulate services that meet the educational needs of the students who have been identified. As Shore, Cornell, Robinson, and Ward (1991) expressed, "Once the child is admitted, performance is always more important than the entry criterion or score" (p. 55).

REFERENCES

Argulewicz, E. N., Elliot, S. N., & Hall, R. (1982). Comparison of behavioral ratings of Anglo-American and Mexican-American gifted children. *Psychology in the Schools, 19,* 469-472.

Ashman, S. S., & Vukelich, C. (1983). The effect of different types of nomination forms on teachers' identification of gifted children. *Psychology in the Schools, 20,* 518-527.

Borland, J. (1978). Teacher identification of the gifted: A new look. *Journal for the Education of the Gifted, 2,* 22-32.

Burke, J. P., Haworth, C. E., & Ware, W. B. (1982). Scales for Rating the Behavioral Characteristics of Superior Students: An investigation of factor structure. *Journal of Special Education, 16,* 477-485.

Busse, T. V., Dahme, G., Wagner, H., & Wieczerkowski, H. (1986). Factors underlying teacher perceptions of highly gifted students: A cross-cultural study. *Educational and Psychological Measurement, 46,* 905-915.

Cronbach, L. J. (1971). Test validation. In R. L. Thorndike (Ed.), *Educational measurement* (2nd ed.). Washington, DC: American Council in Education.

Cummings, W. B. (1980). *Cummings checklist of characteristics of gifted and talented children.* Philadelphia, PA: Annual International Convention of the Council for Exceptional Children. (ERIC Document Reproduction Service No. ED 187 065)

Davis, G., A., & Rimm, S. B. (1994). *Education of the gifted and talented* (3rd ed.). Boston: Allyn & Bacon.

Elliot, S. N., Argulewicz, E. N., & Turco, T. L. (1986). Predictive validity of the Scales for Rating the Behavioral Characteristics of Superior Students for gifted children from three sociocultural groups. *Journal of Experimental Education, 55,* 27-32.

Feldhusen, J. F., Asher, J. W., & Hoover, S. M. (1984). Problems in the identification of giftedness, talent, or ability. *Gifted Child Quarterly, 28,* 149-151.

Friedman, T. C., & Murphy, D. L. (1992). *Assessing the construct validity of the Scales for Rating the Behavioral Characteristics of Superior Students.* Unpublished manuscript. University of Kansas.

Gable, R. K., & Wolf, M. B. (1993). *Instrument development in the affective domain: Measuring attitudes and values in corporate and school settings* (2nd ed.). Boston: Kluwer Academic Publications.

Glassnapp, D. R., Kros, D. S., Isaac, R., Hitz, J., & Carlton, R. (1981). *Use of discriminate analysis in the identification of gifted students.* NY: Annual International Convention of the Council for Exceptional Children. (ERIC Document Reproduction Service No. ED 209 823)

Gridley, B. E. (1984). Construct validity of the Scales for Rating the Behavioral Characteristics of Superior Students: A confirmatory factor analysis. *Dissertation Abstracts International, 45,* 3307-A. (University Microfilms No. DA8425154)

Harty, H., Adkins D. M., & Sherwood, R. D. (1984). Predictability of giftedness identification indices for two recognized approaches to elementary school gifted education. *Journal of Educational Research, 77,* 337-342.

Hunter, J. A., & Lowe, J. D. (1978). The use of the WISC-R, Otis, Iowa, and SRBCSS in identifying gifted elementary children. *Southern Journal of Educational Research, 12,* 59-65.

Kalantan, A. R. (1991*). The effects of inservice training on Bahraini teachers' perceptions of giftedness.* Unpublished doctoral dissertation. University of Connecticut.

Karnes, F. A., Chauvin, J. D., & Trant, T. J. (1984). Leadership profiles as determined by the HSPQ of students identified as intellectually gifted. *Roeper Review, 7,* 46-48.

Kysilka, M. L., Ferguson, M., Wiles, M., Johene, S. M., & Jean, S. M. (1979). *A preliminary study to determine the validity of the Annehurst Curriculum Classification System as a means of identifying gifted/talented students.* San Francisco: American Educational Research Association. (ERIC Document Reproduction Service No. ED 173 985)

Lowrance, D., & Anderson, H. M. (1977). *Intercorrelation of the WISC-R and the Renzulli-Hartman scale for determination of gifted placement.* Atlanta, GA: Annual International Convention of the Council for Exceptional Children. (ERIC Document Reproduction Service No. ED 139 140)

Mayfield, B. (1979). Teacher perception of creativity, intelligence and achievement. *Gifted Child Quarterly, 23,* 812-817.

Nitko, A. J. (1996). *Educational assessment of students* (2nd ed.). New York: Merrill/Prentice Hall.

Perrone, P., & Chen, F. (1982). Toward the development of an identification instrument for the gifted. *Roeper Review, 5,* 45-48.

Popham, W. J. (1995). *Classroom assessment: What teachers need to know.* Boston: Allyn and Bacon.

Purcell, J. H., & Renzulli, J. S. (1998). *The total talent portfolio.* Mansfield Center, CT: Creative Learning Press.

Renzulli, J. S. (1990). A practical system for identifying gifted and talented students. *Early Childhood Development, 63,* 9-18. (Also available on-line at http://www.sp.uconn.edu/~nrcgt/sem/semart04.html.)

Renzulli, J. S., Smith, L. H., White, A. J., Callahan, C. M., & Hartman, R. K. (1976). *Scales for rating the behavioral characteristics of superior students.* Mansfield Center, CT: Creative Learning Press, Inc.

Renzulli, J. S., & Delcourt, M. A. B. (1986). The legacy and logic of research on the identification of gifted persons. *Gifted Child Quarterly, 30,* 20-23.

Renzulli, J. S., & Reis, S. M. (1997). *The schoolwide enrichment model* (2nd ed.). Mansfield Center, CT: Creative Learning Press.

Renzulli, J. S., & Westberg, K. L. (1991). *Rating student performance in a gifted program.* Unpublished instrument. The National Research Center on the Gifted and Talented, University of Connecticut.

Rust, J. D., & Lose, B. D. (1980). Screening for giftedness with the Slosson and the Scales for Rating the Behavioral Characteristics of Superior Students. *Psychology in the Schools, 17,* 446-451.

Singer, E. M., Houtz, J. C., & Rosenfield, S. (1992). Teacher-identified characteristics of successful gifted students: A delphi study. *Educational Research Quarterly, 15*(3), 5-15.

Shore, B. M., Cornell, D. G., Robinson, A., & Ward, V. S. (1991). *Recommended practices in gifted education: A critical analysis.* NY: Teachers College Press.

SPSS Inc. (1988). *SPSS-X user's guide.* Chicago: Author.

Srour, N. H. (1989). *An analysis of teacher judgment in the identification of gifted Jordanian students.* Unpublished doctoral dissertation, University of Connecticut.

Subhi, T. (1997). Who is gifted? A computerised identification procedure. *High Ability Students, 8*(2), 189-211.

Swenson, E. V. (1978). Teacher-assessment of creative behavior in disadvantaged children. *Gifted Child Quarterly, 22,* 338-343.

APPENDICES

Appendix A

Second Field Test Version

TEACHER JUDGMENT OF STUDENT CHARACTERISTICS

A REVISION OF THE *SCALES FOR RATING THE BEHAVIORAL CHARACTERISTICS OF SUPERIOR STUDENTS*

Directions: Please complete the following rating scale on each of your above-average students. The rating form below contains items that are designed to obtain teachers' estimates of student characteristics in the areas of learning, motivation, creativity and leadership. The ratings for each item should reflect the frequency to which you have observed each characteristic. Strict confidentiality will be maintained on all students and teachers who complete this rating form. Your assistance in completing this rating form is greatly appreciated!

Instructions: Please read each item below and **circle** the number that corresponds with the frequency to which you have observed each behavior. Note: Each item should be read with the beginning phrase, **The student demonstrates . . . .** The words that correspond to the six scale values are:

Never	Very Rarely	Rarely	Occasionally	Frequently	Always
1	2	3	4	5	6

Student's Name (or Assigned Code No.)_____

LEARNING CHARACTERISTICS

The student demonstrates . . .

1. advanced vocabulary for his or her age or grade level.   1   2   3   4   5   6

2. the ability to make generalizations about events, people, and things.   1   2   3   4   5   6

3. a large storehouse of information about a specific topic.   1   2   3   4   5   6

4. the ability to grasp underlying principles.   1   2   3   4   5   6

5. interest in many "adult" topics, such as religion, politics, race and ethics.   1   2   3   4   5   6

6. insight into cause and effect relationships.   1   2   3   4   5   6

Never	Very Rarely	Rarely	Occasionally	Frequently	Always
1	2	3	4	5	6

7. an understanding of complicated material through analytical reasoning ability. 1 2 3 4 5 6

8. a large storehouse of information about a variety of topics. 1 2 3 4 5 6

9. the ability to deal with abstractions. 1 2 3 4 5 6

10. recall of factual information. 1 2 3 4 5 6

11. keen and insightful observations. 1 2 3 4 5 6

12. the ability to state and define goals and priorities of others even when they are not the same as his or her own. 1 2 3 4 5 6

13. the ability to transfer learnings from one situation to another. 1 2 3 4 5 6

CREATIVITY CHARACTERISTICS

The student demonstrates . . .

14. imaginative thinking ability. 1 2 3 4 5 6

15. a sense of humor. 1 2 3 4 5 6

16. the ability to come up with unusual, unique, or clever responses. 1 2 3 4 5 6

17. sensitivity to beauty and the aesthetic characteristics of things. 1 2 3 4 5 6

18. an adventurous spirit or a willingness to take risks. 1 2 3 4 5 6

19. the ability to generate a large number of ideas or solutions to problems or questions. 1 2 3 4 5 6

20. a tendency to see humor in situations that may not appear to be humorous to others. 1 2 3 4 5 6

21. the ability to adapt, improve, or modify objects or ideas. 1 2 3 4 5 6

22. the ability to generate ideas that fall into different categories. 1 2 3 4 5 6

23. intellectual playfulness, willingness to fantasize and manipulate ideas. 1 2 3 4 5 6

24. a non-conforming attitude, does not fear being different. 1 2 3 4 5 6

Never	Very Rarely	Rarely	Occasionally	Frequently	Always
1	2	3	4	5	6

MOTIVATION CHARACTERISTICS

The student demonstrates . . .

25. the ability to concentrate intently on a topic for a long period of time. 1 2 3 4 5 6

26. behavior that requires little direction from teachers. 1 2 3 4 5 6

27. sustained interest in certain topics or problems. 1 2 3 4 5 6

28. tenacity for finding out information on topics of interest. 1 2 3 4 5 6

29. persistent work on tasks even when setbacks occur. 1 2 3 4 5 6

30. a preference for situations in which he or she can take personal responsibility for the outcomes of his or her efforts. 1 2 3 4 5 6

31. follow-through behavior when interested in a topic or problem. 1 2 3 4 5 6

32. intense involvement in certain topics or problems. 1 2 3 4 5 6

33. a commitment to long term projects when interested in a topic. 1 2 3 4 5 6

34. persistence when pursuing goals. 1 2 3 4 5 6

35. little need for external motivation to follow through in work that is initially exciting. 1 2 3 4 5 6

LEADERSHIP CHARACTERISTICS

The student demonstrates . . .

36. responsible behavior, can be counted on to follow through on activities/projects. 1 2 3 4 5 6

37. a tendency to be respected by classmates. 1 2 3 4 5 6

38. the ability to articulate ideas and communicate well with others. 1 2 3 4 5 6

39. self-confidence when interacting with age peers. 1 2 3 4 5 6

40. the ability to organize and bring structure to things, people, and situations. 1 2 3 4 5 6

41. cooperative behavior when working with others. 1 2 3 4 5 6

Never	Very Rarely	Rarely	Occasionally	Frequently	Always
1	2	3	4	5	6

42. a tendency to direct an activity when he or she is involved with others.　　　1　2　3　4　5　6

43. verbal behavior characterized by "richness" of expression, elaboration, and fluency.　　　1　2　3　4　5　6

Thank You for Your Time!

Appendix B

Rating Student Performance in a Gifted Program

J. S. Renzulli & K. L. Westberg
The University of Connecticut, 1991

DIRECTIONS: Please complete the following rating scale on each of your students. The form below contains items that are designed to obtain the gifted education teacher's rating of the student's participation in the gifted education program during the school year.

INSTRUCTIONS: Please read each item below and **circle** the number that corresponds with the degree to which you have observed each behavior. Note: each item should be read with the beginning phrase, **This year, the student . . . .** The words that correspond to the six scale values are:

Not Applicable	Very Low Degree	Low Degree	Moderate Degree	High Degree	Very High Degree
0	1	2	3	4	5

Student's Name (or Assigned Code No.) _____ Grade Level _____

This year, the student . . .

	Not Applicable	Very Low Degree	Low Degree	Moderate Degree	High Degree	Very High Degree
1. demonstrated enthusiasm and involvement in gifted education program activities.	0	1	2	3	4	5
2. demonstrated effective use of creative thinking and creative problem solving processes.	0	1	2	3	4	5
3. contributed ideas and information to group discussions.	0	1	2	3	4	5
4. demonstrated effective use of critical thinking skills.	0	1	2	3	4	5
5. created quality products.	0	1	2	3	4	5
6. pursued challenging activities.	0	1	2	3	4	5
7. demonstrated effective written, oral, or visual communication skills.	0	1	2	3	4	5
8. interacted in a positive way with other students.	0	1	2	3	4	5
9. used appropriate research skills to solve problems.	0	1	2	3	4	5
10. demonstrated overall success in the gifted education program.	0	1	2	3	4	5

Appendix C

SCALES FOR RATING THE BEHAVIORAL CHARACTERISTICS OF SUPERIOR STUDENTS

Joseph S. Renzulli / Linda H. Smith / Alan J. White / Carolyn M. Callahan / Robert K. Hartman / Karen L. Westberg

Directions: These scales are designed to obtain teacher estimates of a student's characteristics in the areas of Learning, Motivation, Creativity, Leadership, Art, Music, Drama, Communication, and Planning. The items are derived from the research literature dealing with characteristics of gifted and creative individuals. It should be pointed out that a considerable amount of individual differences can be found within this population, and therefore, the profiles are likely to vary a great deal. Each item in the scales should be considered separately and should reflect the degree to which you have observed the presence or absence of each characteristic. Since the ten dimensions of the instrument represent relatively different sets of behaviors, the scores obtained from the separate scales should *not* be summed to yield a total score. In addition, we have purposefully avoided developing national norms for this instrument. If you choose to develop local norms, they should be constructed for individual schools and grade levels.

Read each item in each scale and place an "X" in the box that corresponds with the frequency to which you have observed the behavior. Each item should be read with the beginning phrase, **"The student demonstrates . . ."** or **"The student . . ."**

Scoring:
- Add the total number of **X**'s in each column to obtain the "Column Total."
- Multiply the "Column Total" by the "Weight" for each column to obtain the "Weighted Column Total."
- Sum the "Weighted Column Totals" across to obtain the Score for each dimension of the scale.
- Enter the Scores below.

I	Learning Characteristics	_____
II	Creativity Characteristics	_____
III	Motivation Characteristics	_____
IV	Leadership Characteristics	_____
V	Artistic Characteristics	_____
VI	Musical Characteristics	_____
VII	Dramatics Characteristics	_____
VIII	Communication Characteristics (Precision)	_____
IX	Communication Characteristics (Expressiveness)	_____
X	Planning Characteristics	_____

© 2002. *Scales for Rating the Behavioral Characteristics of Superior Students.* Creative Learning Press, Inc. All Rights Reserved.

LEARNING CHARACTERISTICS

The student demonstrates . . .

	Never	Very Rarely	Rarely	Occasionally	Frequently	Always
1. advanced vocabulary for his or her age or grade level.	☐	☐	☐	☐	☐	☐
2. the ability to make generalizations about events, people, and things.	☐	☐	☐	☐	☐	☐
3. a large storehouse of information about a specific topic.	☐	☐	☐	☐	☐	☐
4. the ability to grasp underlying principles.	☐	☐	☐	☐	☐	☐
5. insight into cause and effect relationships.	☐	☐	☐	☐	☐	☐
6. an understanding of complicated material through analytical reasoning ability.	☐	☐	☐	☐	☐	☐
7. a large storehouse of information about a variety of topics	☐	☐	☐	☐	☐	☐
8. the ability to deal with abstractions.	☐	☐	☐	☐	☐	☐
9. recall of factual information.	☐	☐	☐	☐	☐	☐
10. keen and insightful observations.	☐	☐	☐	☐	☐	☐
11. the ability to transfer learning from one situation to another.	☐	☐	☐	☐	☐	☐
Add Column Total	☐	☐	☐	☐	☐	☐
Multiply by Weight	1	2	3	4	5	6
Add Weighted Column Totals	☐ +	☐ +	☐ +	☐ +	☐ +	☐
Scale Total						☐

CREATIVITY CHARACTERISTICS

The student demonstrates . . .

	Never	Very Rarely	Rarely	Occasionally	Frequently	Always
1. imaginative thinking ability.	☐	☐	☐	☐	☐	☐
2. a sense of humor.	☐	☐	☐	☐	☐	☐
3. the ability to come up with unusual, unique, or clever responses.	☐	☐	☐	☐	☐	☐
4. an adventurous spirit or a willingness to take risks.	☐	☐	☐	☐	☐	☐
5. the ability to generate a large number of ideas or solutions to problems or questions.	☐	☐	☐	☐	☐	☐
6. a tendency to see humor in situations that may not appear to be humorous to others.	☐	☐	☐	☐	☐	☐
7. the ability to adapt, improve, or modify objects or ideas.	☐	☐	☐	☐	☐	☐
8. intellectual playfulness, willingness to fantasize and manipulate ideas.	☐	☐	☐	☐	☐	☐
9. a non-conforming attitude, does not fear being different.	☐	☐	☐	☐	☐	☐
Add Column Total	☐	☐	☐	☐	☐	☐
Multiply by Weight	1	2	3	4	5	6
Add Weighted Column Totals	☐ +	☐ +	☐ +	☐ +	☐ +	☐
Scale Total						☐

SAMPLE

MOTIVATION CHARACTERISTICS

The student demonstrates . . .

	Never	Very Rarely	Rarely	Occasionally	Frequently	Always
1. the ability to concentrate intently on a topic for a long period of time.	☐	☐	☐	☐	☐	☐
2. behavior that requires little direction from teachers.	☐	☐	☐	☐	☐	☐
3. sustained interest in certain topics or problems.	☐	☐	☐	☐	☐	☐
4. tenacity for finding out information on topics of interest.	☐	☐	☐	☐	☐	☐
5. persistent work on tasks even when setbacks occur.	☐	☐	☐	☐	☐	☐
6. a preference for situations in which he or she can take personal responsibility for the outcomes of his or her efforts.	☐	☐	☐	☐	☐	☐
7. follow-through behavior when interested in a topic or problem.	☐	☐	☐	☐	☐	☐
8. intense involvement in certain topics or problems.	☐	☐	☐	☐	☐	☐
9. a commitment to long term projects when interested in a topic.	☐	☐	☐	☐	☐	☐
10. persistence when pursuing goals.	☐	☐	☐	☐	☐	☐
11. little need for external motivation to follow through in work that is initially exciting.	☐	☐	☐	☐	☐	☐
Add Column Total	☐	☐	☐	☐	☐	☐
Multiply by Weight	1	2	3	4	5	6
Add Weighted Column Totals	☐ +	☐ +	☐ +	☐ +	☐ +	☐
Scale Total						☐

LEADERSHIP CHARACTERISTICS

The student demonstrates . . .

	Never	Very Rarely	Rarely	Occasionally	Frequently	Always
1. responsible behavior, can be counted on to follow through on activities/projects.	☐	☐	☐	☐	☐	☐
2. a tendency to be respected by classmates.	☐	☐	☐	☐	☐	☐
3. the ability to articulate ideas and communicate well with others.	☐	☐	☐	☐	☐	☐
4. self-confidence when interacting with age peers.	☐	☐	☐	☐	☐	☐
5. the ability to organize and bring structure to things, people, and situations.	☐	☐	☐	☐	☐	☐
6. cooperative behavior when working with others.	☐	☐	☐	☐	☐	☐
7. a tendency to direct an activity when he or she is involved with others.	☐	☐	☐	☐	☐	☐
Add Column Total	☐	☐	☐	☐	☐	☐
Multiply by Weight	1	2	3	4	5	6
Add Weighted Column Totals	☐ +	☐ +	☐ +	☐ +	☐ +	☐
Scale Total						☐

ARTISTIC CHARACTERISTICS

The student . . .

	Never	Very Rarely	Rarely	Occasionally	Frequently	Always
1. likes to participate in art activities; is eager to visually express ideas.	☐	☐	☐	☐	☐	☐
2. incorporates a large number of elements into art work; varies the subject and content of art work.	☐	☐	☐	☐	☐	☐
3. arrives at unique, unconventional solutions to artistic problems as opposed to traditional, conventional ones.	☐	☐	☐	☐	☐	☐
4. concentrates for long periods of time on art projects.	☐	☐	☐	☐	☐	☐
5. willingly tries out different media; experiments with a variety of materials and techniques.	☐	☐	☐	☐	☐	☐
6. tends to select art media for free activity or classroom projects.	☐	☐	☐	☐	☐	☐
7. is particularly sensitive to the environment; is a keen observer—sees the unusual, what may be overlooked by others.	☐	☐	☐	☐	☐	☐
8. produces balance and order in art work.	☐	☐	☐	☐	☐	☐
9. is critical of his or her own work; sets high standards of quality; often reworks creation in order to refine it.	☐	☐	☐	☐	☐	☐
10. shows an interest in other students' work—spends time studying and discussing their work.	☐	☐	☐	☐	☐	☐
11. elaborates on ideas from other people—uses them as a "jumping-off point" as opposed to copying them.	☐	☐	☐	☐	☐	☐
Add Column Total	☐	☐	☐	☐	☐	☐
Multiply by Weight	1	2	3	4	5	6
Add Weighted Column Totals	☐ +	☐ +	☐ +	☐ +	☐ +	☐
Scale Total						☐

MUSICAL CHARACTERISTICS

The student . . .

	Never	Very Rarely	Rarely	Occasionally	Frequently	Always
1. shows a sustained interest in music—seeks out opportunities to hear and create music.	☐	☐	☐	☐	☐	☐
2. perceives fine differences in musical tone (pitch, loudness, timbre, duration).	☐	☐	☐	☐	☐	☐
3. easily remembers melodies and can produce them accurately.	☐	☐	☐	☐	☐	☐
4. eagerly participates in musical activities.	☐	☐	☐	☐	☐	☐
5. plays a musical instrument (or indicates a strong desire to).	☐	☐	☐	☐	☐	☐
6. is sensitive to the rhythm of music; responds to changes in the tempo of music through body movements.	☐	☐	☐	☐	☐	☐
7. is aware of and can identify a variety of sounds heard at a given moment—is sensitive to "background" noises, to chords that accompany a melody, to the different sounds of singers or instrumentalists in a performance.	☐	☐	☐	☐	☐	☐

Add Column Total

☐	☐	☐	☐	☐	☐

Multiply by Weight

1	2	3	4	5	6

Add Weighted Column Totals

☐ + ☐ + ☐ + ☐ + ☐ + ☐

Scale Total

☐

DRAMATICS CHARACTERISTICS

The student . . .

	Never	Very Rarely	Rarely	Occasionally	Frequently	Always
1. volunteers to participate in classroom plays or skits.	☐	☐	☐	☐	☐	☐
2. easily tells a story or gives an account of some experience.	☐	☐	☐	☐	☐	☐
3. effectively uses gestures and facial expressions to communicate feelings.	☐	☐	☐	☐	☐	☐
4. is adept at role-playing, improvising, acting out situations "on the spot."	☐	☐	☐	☐	☐	☐
5. can readily identify himself or herself with the moods and motivations of characters.	☐	☐	☐	☐	☐	☐
6. handles body with ease and poise for his or her particular age.	☐	☐	☐	☐	☐	☐
7. creates original plays or makes up plays from stories.	☐	☐	☐	☐	☐	☐
8. commands and holds the attention of a group when speaking.	☐	☐	☐	☐	☐	☐
9. is able to evoke emotional responses from listeners—can get people to laugh, frown, feel tense, etc.	☐	☐	☐	☐	☐	☐
10. can imitate others—is able to mimic the way people speak, walk, gesture.	☐	☐	☐	☐	☐	☐
Add Column Total	☐	☐	☐	☐	☐	☐
Multiply by Weight	1	2	3	4	5	6
Add Weighted Column Totals	☐ +	☐ +	☐ +	☐ +	☐ +	☐
Scale Total						☐

COMMUNICATION CHARACTERISTICS (PRECISION)

The student . . .

	Never	Very Rarely	Rarely	Occasionally	Frequently	Always
1. speaks and writes directly and to the point.	□	□	□	□	□	□
2. modifies and adjusts expression of ideas for maximum reception.	□	□	□	□	□	□
3. is able to revise and edit in a way which is concise, yet retains essential ideas.	□	□	□	□	□	□
4. explains things precisely and clearly.	□	□	□	□	□	□
5. uses descriptive words to add color, emotion, and beauty.	□	□	□	□	□	□
6. expresses thoughts and needs clearly and concisely.	□	□	□	□	□	□
7. can find various ways of expressing ideas so others will understand.	□	□	□	□	□	□
8. can describe things in a few very appropriate words.	□	□	□	□	□	□
9. is able to express fine shades of meaning by using a large stock of synonyms.	□	□	□	□	□	□
10. is able to express ideas in a variety of alternate ways.	□	□	□	□	□	□
11. knows and can use many words closely related in meaning.	□	□	□	□	□	□
Add Column Total	□	□	□	□	□	□
Multiply by Weight	1	2	3	4	5	6
Add Weighted Column Totals	□ +	□ +	□ +	□ +	□ +	□
Scale Total						□

COMMUNICATION CHARACTERISTICS (EXPRESSIVENESS)

The student . . .

	Never	Very Rarely	Rarely	Occasionally	Frequently	Always
1. uses voice expressively to convey or enhance meaning.	☐	☐	☐	☐	☐	☐
2. conveys information non-verbally through gestures, facial expressions, and "body language."	☐	☐	☐	☐	☐	☐
3. is an interesting storyteller.	☐	☐	☐	☐	☐	☐
4. uses colorful and imaginative figures of speech such as puns and analogies.	☐	☐	☐	☐	☐	☐
Add Column Total	☐	☐	☐	☐	☐	☐
Multiply by Weight	1	2	3	4	5	6
Add Weighted Column Totals	☐ +	☐ +	☐ +	☐ +	☐ +	☐
Scale Total						☐

PLANNING CHARACTERISTICS

The student . . .

		Never	Very Rarely	Rarely	Occasionally	Frequently	Always
1.	determines what information or resources are necessary for accomplishing a task.	☐	☐	☐	☐	☐	☐
2.	grasps the relationship of individual steps to a whole process.	☐	☐	☐	☐	☐	☐
3.	allows time to execute all steps involved in a process.	☐	☐	☐	☐	☐	☐
4.	foresees consequences or effects of action.	☐	☐	☐	☐	☐	☐
5.	organizes his or her work well.	☐	☐	☐	☐	☐	☐
6.	takes into account the details necessary to accomplish a goal.	☐	☐	☐	☐	☐	☐
7.	is good at games of strategy where it is necessary to anticipate several moves ahead.	☐	☐	☐	☐	☐	☐
8.	recognizes the various alternative methods for accomplishing a goal.	☐	☐	☐	☐	☐	☐
9.	can pinpoint where areas of difficulty might arise in a procedure or activity.	☐	☐	☐	☐	☐	☐
10.	arranges steps of a project in a sensible order or time sequence.	☐	☐	☐	☐	☐	☐
11.	is good at breaking down an activity into step-by-step procedures.	☐	☐	☐	☐	☐	☐
12.	establishes priorities when organizing activities.	☐	☐	☐	☐	☐	☐
13.	shows awareness of limitations relating to time, space, materials, and abilities when working on group or individual projects.	☐	☐	☐	☐	☐	☐
14.	can provide details that contribute to the development of a plan or procedure.	☐	☐	☐	☐	☐	☐
15.	sees alternative ways to distribute work or assign people to accomplish a task.	☐	☐	☐	☐	☐	☐

SAMPLE

Add Column Total	☐	☐	☐	☐	☐	☐
Multiply by Weight	1	2	3	4	5	6
Add Weighted Column Totals	☐ +	☐ +	☐ +	☐ +	☐ +	☐

Scale Total ☐

Appendix D

Teacher Training Exercise for
Completing the *Scales for Rating the Behavioral Characteristics of Superior Students-R (SRBCSS-R)*

LEARNING CHARACTERISTICS

TASK No. 1: Individually, select the letter of a key concept that you believe most closely matches each item.

TASK No. 2: In a small group, discuss specific examples of when you have observed each behavior in a student.

Key Concepts		
A. Analytical	E. Conceptual Understanding	I. Inductive
B. Knowledgeable	F. Widely Knowledgeable	J. Articulate
C. Applied Thinking	G. Reasoning Ability	K. Insightful
D. Memory	H. Abstract Thinking	

The student demonstrates . . .

1. advanced vocabulary for his or her age or grade level. _____

2. the ability to make generalizations about events, people, and things. _____

3. a large storehouse of information about a specific topic. _____

4. the ability to grasp underlying principles. _____

5. insight into cause and effect relationships. _____

6. an understanding of complicated material through analytical reasoning ability. _____

7. a large storehouse of information about a variety of topics. _____

8. the ability to deal with abstractions. _____

9. recall of factual information. _____

10. keen and insightful observations. _____

11. the ability to transfer learnings from one situation to another. _____

Teacher Training Exercise for
Completing the *Scales for Rating the Behavioral Characteristics of Superior Students-R (SRBCSS-R)*

CREATIVITY CHARACTERISTICS

TASK No. 1: Individually, select the letter of a key concept that you believe most closely matches each item.

TASK No. 2: In a small group, discuss specific examples of when you have observed each behavior in a student.

Key Concepts		
A. Flexible Thinker	D. Astute	G. Original Thinker
B. Imaginative	E. Non-Conformist	H. Fluent Thinker
C. Risk-Taker	F. Mentally Mischievous	I. Witty

The student demonstrates . . .

1. imaginative thinking ability. _____

2. a sense of humor. _____

3. the ability to come up with unusual, unique, or clever responses. _____

4. an adventurous spirit or a willingness to take risks. _____

5. the ability to generate a large number of ideas or solutions to problems or questions. _____

6. a tendency to see humor in situations that may not appear to be humorous to others. _____

7. the ability to adapt, improve, or modify objects or ideas. _____

8. intellectual playfulness, willingness to fantasize, and manipulate ideas. _____

9. a non-conforming attitude, does not fear being different. _____

Teacher Training Exercise for
Completing the *Scales for Rating the Behavioral Characteristics of Superior Students-R (SRBCSS-R)*

MOTIVATION CHARACTERISTICS

TASK No. 1: Individually, select the letter of a key concept that you believe most closely matches each item.

TASK No. 2: In a small group, discuss specific examples of when you have observed each behavior in a student.

Key Concepts

A. Goal Directed	E. Intrinsically Motivated	I. Totally Consumed
B. Unwavering Drive	F. Task Committed	J. Dogged Pursuit
C. Self-Directed	G. Focused Concentration	K. Unyielding
D. Self-Reliant	H. Continuously Intrigued	Inquisitiveness

The student demonstrates . . .

1. the ability to concentrate intently on a topic for a long period of time. _____

2. behavior that requires little direction from teachers. _____

3. sustained interest in certain topics or problems. _____

4. tenacity for finding out information on topics of interest. _____

5. persistent work on tasks even when setbacks occur. _____

6. a preference for situations in which he or she can take personal responsibility for the outcomes of his or her efforts. _____

7. follow-through behavior when interested in a topic or problem. _____

8. intense involvement in certain topics or problems. _____

9. a commitment to long term projects when interested in a topic. _____

10. persistence when pursuing goals. _____

11. little need for external motivation to follow through in work that is initially exciting. _____

Teacher Training Exercise for
Completing the *Scales for Rating the Behavioral Characteristics of Superior Students-R (SRBCSS-R)*

LEADERSHIP CHARACTERISTICS

TASK No. 1: Individually, select the letter of a key concept that you believe most closely matches each item.

TASK No. 2: In a small group, discuss specific examples of when you have observed each behavior in a student.

Key Concepts

A. Poised   D. Facilitator   F. Director
B. Dependable   E. Highly Regarded   G. Articulate
C. Collaborative

The student demonstrates . . .

1. responsible behavior; can be counted on to follow through on activities/projects. _____

2. a tendency to be respected by classmates. _____

3. the ability to articulate ideas and communicate well with others. _____

4. self-confidence when interacting with age peers. _____

5. the ability to organize and bring structure to things, people, and situations. _____

6. cooperative behavior when working with others. _____

7. a tendency to direct an activity when he or she is involved with others. _____

Suggested Answer Key for the Teacher Training Exercise
for Completing the *Scales for Rating the Behavioral Characteristics of Superior Students-R* (SRBCSS-R)

LEARNING CHARACTERISTICS

1. J
2. I
3. B
4. E

5. G
6. A
7. F
8. H

9. D
10. K
11. C

CREATIVITY CHARACTERISTICS

1. B
2. I
3. G

4. C
5. H
6. D

7. A
8. F
9. E

MOTIVATION CHARACTERISTICS

1. G
2. C
3. H
4. K

5. B
6. D
7. J
8. I

9. F
10. A
11. E

LEADERSHIP CHARACTERISTICS

1. B
2. E
3. G

4. A
5. D

6. C
7. F

Appendix E

Calculating Local Percentile Rank Norms

1. List the possible scores in descending order (Column 1). (You may group the scores into intervals if you wish.)
2. Tally the number of students attaining each score (Column 2).
3. Sum the number of students attaining each score (Column 3).
4. Add the frequencies consecutively, starting at the bottom of the column with the lowest score. Place each consecutive sum in the cumulative frequency column (Column 4) (e.g., $0 + 1 = 1, \ldots, 2 + 1 = 3, 3 + 2 = 5$, etc.). These cumulative frequencies are the number of students at and below each particular score.
5. Calculate the percentile rank of each score (Column 5). Below is an example for a score of 27.
   (a) Calculate one-half of the frequency of the score ($1/2 \times 5 = 2.5$).
   (b) Add the result in (a) to the cumulative frequency just below the score (e.g., $2.5 + 11 = 13.5$).
   (c) Divide the result in (b) by the total number of scores ($13.5 \div 25 = .54$).
   (d) Multiply the result in (c) by 100 ($.54 \times 100 = 54$).

Raw	Tally	Frequency	Cumulative Frequency	Percentile Rank $\dfrac{1/2(\#\text{ of persons with the score}) + \#\text{ of persons below the score}}{\text{total number of persons}}$
36	/	1	25	$98 = \dfrac{1/2(1) + 24}{25} \times 100$
35		0	24	96
34		0	24	96
33		0	24	$96 = \dfrac{1/2(0) + 24}{25} \times 100$
32	/	1	24	$94 = \dfrac{1/2(1) + 23}{25} \times 100$
31	/	1	23	$90 = \dfrac{1/2(1) + 22}{25} \times 100$
30		0	22	$88 = \dfrac{1/2(0) + 22}{25} \times 100$
29	//	2	22	$84 = \dfrac{1/2(2) + 20}{25} \times 100$
28	////	4	20	$72 = \dfrac{1/2(4) + 16}{25} \times 100$
27	/////	5	16	$54 = \dfrac{1/2(5) + 11}{25} \times 100$
26	///// /	6	11	$32 = \dfrac{1/2(6) + 5}{25} \times 100$
25	//	2	5	$16 = \dfrac{1/2(2) + 3}{25} \times 100$
24	/	1	3	$10 = \dfrac{1/2(1) + 2}{25} \times 100$
23		0	2	8
22		0	2	$8 = \dfrac{1/2(0) + 2}{25} \times 100$
21	/	1	2	$6 = \dfrac{1/2(1) + 1}{25} \times 100$
19		0	1	4
18		0	1	4
17		0	1	4
16		0	1	4
15		0	1	$4 = \dfrac{1/2(0) + 1}{25} \times 100$
14	/	1	1	$2 = \dfrac{1/2(1) + 0}{25} \times 100$

$N = 25$

Source: Nitko, A. J. (1996). *Educational assessment of students* (2nd ed.). New York: Merrill/Prentice Hall.

Appendix F
A Practical System for Identifying Gifted and Talented Students
by Joseph S. Renzulli

Many schools have struggled to identify needs and provide appropriate services to their students. Many plans for identifying gifted and talented students make use of only very narrow criteria (e.g., test scores), and as a result, they take only an equally narrowly defined population of students. Consequently, many educators have approached me about devising plans that are more flexible—plans that take into consideration students who may not score well on traditional assessments, but who demonstrate potential inside or outside of the school environment.

The system for identifying gifted and talented students described in this article represents efforts to offer alternative avenues for identifying students for special services. It is based on a broad body of research on the characteristics of creative and productive individuals (Renzulli, 1986). This research reveals that highly productive people are characterized by three interlocking clusters of characteristics: above average, though not necessarily superior, ability; task commitment; and creativity. Figure 1 presents a graphic representation of these interlocking clusters, and the following behavioral manifestations of each cluster summarize the major concepts and conclusions emanating from the work of theorists and researchers who have examined these characteristics:

Well Above Average Ability

General Ability

- High levels of abstract thinking, verbal and numerical reasoning, spatial relations, memory, and word fluency.
- Adaptation to the shaping of novel situations encountered in the external environment.
- The automatization of information processing; rapid, accurate, and selective retrieval of information.

Specific Ability

- The application of various combinations of the above general abilities to one or more specialized areas of knowledge or areas of human performance (e.g., the arts, leadership, administration).
- The capacity for acquiring and making appropriate use of advanced amounts of formal knowledge, tacit knowledge, technique, logistics, and strategy in the pursuit of particular problems or the manifestation of specialized areas of performance.
- The capacity to sort out relevant and irrelevant information associated with a particular problem or area of study or performance.

Task Commitment

- The capacity for high levels of interest, enthusiasm, fascination, and involvement in a particular problem, area of study, or form of human expression.

Graphic Representation of the Three-Ring Conception of Giftedness

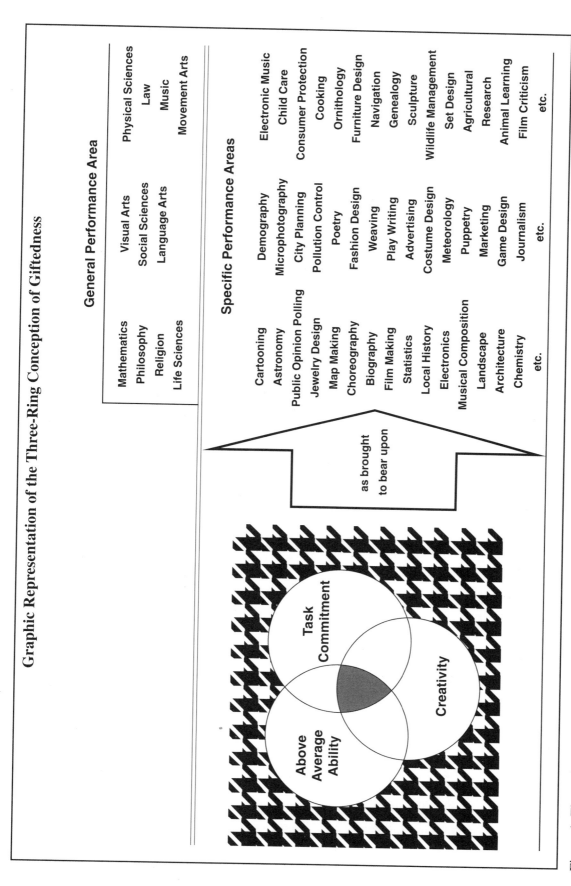

General Performance Area

Mathematics	Visual Arts	Physical Sciences
Philosophy	Social Sciences	Law
Religion	Language Arts	Music
Life Sciences		Movement Arts

Specific Performance Areas

Cartooning	Demography	Electronic Music
Astronomy	Microphotography	Child Care
Public Opinion Polling	City Planning	Consumer Protection
Jewelry Design	Pollution Control	Cooking
Map Making	Poetry	Ornithology
Choreography	Fashion Design	Furniture Design
Biography	Weaving	Navigation
Film Making	Play Writing	Genealogy
Statistics	Advertising	Sculpture
Local History	Costume Design	Wildlife Management
Electronics	Meteorology	Set Design
Musical Composition	Puppetry	Agricultural Research
Landscape Architecture	Marketing	Animal Learning
Chemistry	Game Design	Film Criticism
etc.	Journalism	etc.
	etc.	

as brought to bear upon

Task Commitment

Above Average Ability

Creativity

Figure 1. Three-ring conception of giftedness.

- The capacity for perseverance, endurance, determination, hard work, and dedicated practice.
- Self-confidence, a strong ego and belief in one's ability to carry out important work, freedom from inferiority feelings, drive to achieve.
- The ability to identify significant problems within specialized reason; the ability to tune in to major channels of communication and new developments within given fields.
- Setting high standards for one's work; maintaining an openness to self and external criticism; developing an aesthetic sense of taste, quality, and excellence about one's own work and the work of others.

Creativity

- Fluency, flexibility, and originality of thought.
- Openness to experience; receptive to that which is new and different (even irrational) in thoughts, actions, and products of oneself and others.
- Curious, speculative, adventurous, and "mentally playful"; willing to take risks in thought and action, even to the point of being uninhibited.
- Sensitive to detail, aesthetic characteristics of ideas and things; willing to act on and react to external stimulation and one's own ideas and feelings.

As in any list of traits, there is an overlap among individual items and an interaction between and among the general categories and the specific traits. All the traits do not need to be present in any given individual or situation to produce a display of gifted behaviors. Consequently, the Three-Ring Conception of Giftedness emphasizes the interaction among the clusters rather than any single cluster. However, the above-average-ability cluster is a constant in this identification system. In other words, the well-above-average-ability group represents the target population and the starting point for the identification process, and it will be students in this category that are selected through the use of test score and non-test criteria. Task commitment and creativity are developmental goals of the special program. By providing above-average-ability students with appropriate experiences, the programming model (Renzulli, 1977) for which this identification system was designed serves the purpose of promoting creativity and task commitment and, in "bringing the rings together," promoting the development of gifted behaviors.

This identification system is designed to translate the Three-Ring Conception of Giftedness into a practical set of procedures for selecting students for special programs. The focal point of this identification system is a Talent Pool of students that will serve as the major (but not the only) target group for participation in a wide variety of supplementary services. The three goals of this identification system, as it relates to the Three-Ring Conception of Giftedness, are:

1. To develop creativity and/or task commitment in Talent Pool students and other students who may come to the school's attention through alternate means of identification;
2. To provide learning experiences and support systems that promote the interaction of creativity, task commitment, and above average ability (i.e., to bring the "rings" together);

3. To provide opportunities, resources, and encouragement for the development and application of gifted behaviors.

Before schools begin applying the identification system, they must take into account three important considerations. First, Talent Pools will vary from school to school depending upon the general nature of the total student body. In schools with unusually large numbers of high-ability students, Talent Pools could extend beyond the 15 percent level ordinarily recommended in schools that reflect the achievement profiles of the general population. Even in schools where achievement levels are below national norms, there still exists an upper-level group of students who need services above and beyond those that are provided to the majority of the school population. Some of the most successful SEM programs have been in inner-city schools that serve disadvantaged and bilingual youth. Even though these schools were below national norms, a Talent Pool of approximately 15 percent of higher-ability students needing supplementary services was still identified. Just as Talent Pool size is a function of the student population, it is also a function of the availability of resources (both human and material) and the extent to which the general faculty is willing to (a) make modifications in the regular curriculum for above average ability students, (b) participate in various kinds of enrichment and mentoring activities, and (c) work cooperatively with any and all personnel who may have special program assignments.

Since teacher nomination plays an important role in this identification system, a second consideration is the extent to which teachers have received orientation and training in the program and procedures for nominating students. For teachers who have little or no training, schools should use a training activity that is designed to orient teachers to the behavioral characteristics of superior students in Appendix D of this manual.

A third consideration is, of course, the type of program for which students are being identified. Some avenues for identifying students may be appropriate for some programs and not for others. For example, using creativity assessment tools may not offer information appropriate for identifying students for an accelerated mathematics program. Likewise, schools may wish to rely more heavily on non-test based information when identifying students for a special arts program.

The steps that follow are based on the formation of a 15 percent Talent Pool, but schools can develop larger or smaller Talent Pools by simply adjusting the figures used in this example.

Step 1: Test Score Nominations

Using only test scores to identify a 15 percent Talent Pool would make the identification task quick and easy. Any child who scores above the 85th percentile (using local norms) would be a candidate. However, one of the goals of the identification system described here is to leave some room in the Talent Pool for students whose potentials may not be reflected in standardized tests. Therefore, schools should begin by dividing their Talent Pool in half (see Figure 2) and place all students who score at or above the 92nd percentile (again, using local norms) in the Talent Pool.

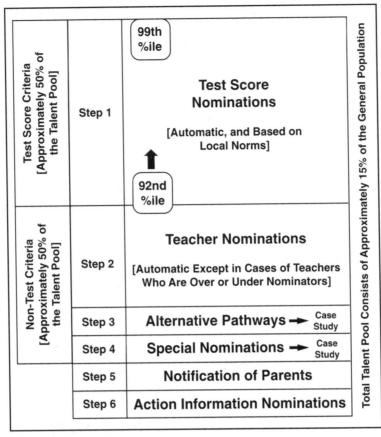

Figure 2. Talent Pool

This approach guarantees that all traditionally bright youngsters will automatically be selected, and they will account for approximately 50 percent of our Talent Pool. This process guarantees admission to bright underachievers.

Schools can use any regularly administered standardized test (e.g., intelligence, achievement, aptitude) for this purpose. However, admission to the Talent Pool should not be granted on the basis of any single test or subtest score. Students who are high in verbal or non-verbal ability, but not necessarily both, will gain admission, as well as students who may excel in one specific aptitude (e.g., spatial, mechanical).

Programs that focus on special areas such as the arts, leadership, and athletics should use non-test criteria as major indicators of above-average ability in a particular talent area. Likewise, whenever test scores are not available, or there is some question as to their validity, schools should employ the non-test criteria recommended in the following steps. This approach (i.e., eliminating or minimizing Step 1) is especially important when considering primary age students, disadvantaged populations, or culturally different groups.

Step 2: Teacher Nominations

After informing teachers of students who gained entrance through test nomination, Step 2 allows teachers to nominate students who display characteristics that are not easily determined by tests (e.g., high levels of creativity, task commitment, unusual interests or talents, or special areas of superior performance or potential). Before teachers nominate students, schools should provide them with some training in recognizing gifted behaviors. With the exception of nominations from teachers who are over-nominators or under-nominators, teacher nominations, then, are accepted into the Talent Pool on an equal value with test score nominations. That is, schools should not refer to students nominated by test scores as the "truly gifted" and students nominated by teachers as the moderately or potentially gifted. Nor should schools make any distinctions in the opportunities, resources, or services provided to students other than the normal individualization that should be a part of any program that attempts to meet unique needs and potentials. Thus, for example, if a student gains entrance on the basis of teacher nomination because he or she has shown advanced potential for creative writing, the student should not compete on an equal basis in mathematics with a student who scored at or above the 92nd percentile on a math test.

Schools can use a teacher nomination form (Renzulli & Reis, 1997, p. 61) and selected scales from the *Scales for Rating the Behavioral Characteristics of Superior Students* for this procedure. Schools should not use the rating scales to eliminate students with lower ratings. Instead, these scales provide a composite profile of the nominated students. In cases of teachers who are over-nominators, schools should ask them to rank their nominations, and the nominations should be reviewed by a schoolwide committee. Step 4 describes procedures for dealing with under-nominators or nonnominators.

Step 3: Alternate Pathways

While all schools using this identification system will use test score and teacher nominations to identify students for services, alternate pathways are local options, and individual schools and districts can pursue them to varying degrees. A local planning committee should decide which alternate pathways the school might use, keeping in mind variations in grade level. For example, self-nomination is more appropriate for students who may be considering advanced classes at the secondary level and not an appropriate alternative for primary-grade students.

Alternate pathways generally consist of parent nominations, peer nominations, tests of creativity, self-nominations, product evaluations, and virtually any other procedure that might lead to initial consideration by a screening committee. The major difference between identification using alternate pathways and test score and teacher nominations is that alternate pathways do not provide automatic admission. In other words, students nominated through one or more alternate pathways will be reviewed by a screening committee, after which the committee makes a selection decision. In most cases the screening committee should carry out a case study that includes examination of all previous school records; interviews with students, teachers, and parents; and any individual assessments recommended by the committee. In some cases, students that are recommended on the basis of one or more alternate pathways can enter the program on a trial basis.

Step 4: Special Nominations (Safety Valve No. 1)

Special nominations represent the first of two safety valves in this identification system. After circulating a list of all students who have been nominated through one of the procedures in Steps 1 through 3 to all teachers within the school and in previous schools (if students have matriculated from another building), previous year teachers can nominate students who have not been recommended by their present teacher, and/or resource teachers can make recommendations based on their own experience with students who have already been in the Talent Pool or students they may have encountered as part of enrichment experiences offered in regular classrooms. These types of nominations after a final review of the total school population are designed to circumvent the opinions of present year teachers who may not have an appreciation for the abilities, style, or even the personality of a particular student. One last sweep through the population also helps to pick up students that may have become "turned-off" to school or developed patterns of underachievement as a result of personal or family problems. In addition, this step helps to overcome the general biases of an under-nominator or a nonnominator. As with the case of alternate pathways, special nominations are not automatic. Rather, a screening committee carries out a case study and makes the final selection decision.

Step 5: Notification and Orientation of Parents

Parents of all Talent Pool students should receive a letter of notification and a comprehensive description of the program. The letter should not indicate that a child has been certified as "gifted." Instead, it should explain the nature of the program and extend an invitation to parents to an orientation meeting. At this meeting, the school should provide a description of the Three-Ring Conception of Giftedness and explain all program policies, procedures, and activities. Parents should learn about how admission to the Talent Pool is determined, that it is carried out on an annual basis, and that additions to Talent Pool membership might take place during the year as a result of evaluations of student participation and progress. Parents should feel free to make individual appointments whenever they want additional information about the program or their own child. Schools should provide a similar orientation session for students, emphasizing once again the services and activities being provided. Students should not be told that they are "the gifted," but through a discussion of the Three-Ring Conception and the procedures for developing general and specific potentials, they should come to understand that the development of gifted behaviors is a program goal as well as part of their own responsibility.

Step 6: Action Information Nominations (Safety Valve No. 2)

In spite of a school's best efforts, this system will occasionally overlook students who, for one reason or another, are not selected for Talent Pool membership. To help overcome this problem, all teachers should receive training related to spotting unusually favorable "turn-ons" in the regular curriculum. Programs following the Schoolwide Enrichment Model (Renzulli & Reis, 1997) will find that they have a wide variety of in-class enrichment experiences that might result in recommendations for special services. A teacher training activity and an instrument called an *Action Information Message* (Renzulli & Reis, 1997) can help facilitate this process.

Action information is best illustrated by the dynamic interactions that occur when a student becomes extremely interested in or excited about a particular topic, area of study, issue, idea or event that takes place inside or outside the school environment. It is derived from the concept of performance based assessment, and it serves as the second safety valve in this identification system. The transmission of an Action Information Message does not mean that a student will automatically revolve into advanced level services. Like the other alternative methods, it serves as the basis for a careful review of the student's situation to determine if services are warranted. (Schools can also use Action Information Messages within Talent Pool settings (i.e., pull-out groups, advanced classes, cluster groups) to make determinations about whether particular students should pursue individual or small group investigations (Type III Enrichment in the Triad Model).)

Toward a More Flexible Identification Approach

In most identification systems that follow the traditional screening-plus-selection approach, the "throw aways" have invariably been those students who qualified for screening on the basis of nontest criteria. Thus, for example, a teacher nomination is used as a ticket to take an individual or group ability test, but in most cases the test score is always the deciding factor. When it comes to the final selection decision, the screening process ignores the many and various "good things" that led to the teacher nominations, and the multiple criteria game ends up being a smoke screen for the same old test-based approach.

The implementation of the identification system described here has helped schools overcome this problem as well as a wide array of other problems traditionally associated with selecting students for special programs. Generally, students, parents, teachers, and administrators have expressed high degrees of satisfaction with this approach (Renzulli, 1988), and the reason for this satisfaction is plainly evident. By picking up that layer of students below the top few percentile levels usually selected for special programs and by leaving room in the program for students to gain entrance on the basis of nontest criteria, schools eliminate the justifiable criticisms of those persons who know that these students are in need of special opportunities, resources, and encouragement. The research underlying the Three-Ring Conception of Giftedness illustrates that such an approach is justified in terms of what is known about human potential. In addition, eliminating the endless number of headaches traditionally associated with identification gains an unprecedented amount of support from teachers and administrators, many of whom, may have formerly resented the very existence of special programs.

As educators begin to implement the identification procedures outlined here, one of the most frequently asked questions is "How will this approach be in line with state guidelines?" Before answering this question, I would like to point out that I have met very few people currently working in special programs who have not expressed dissatisfaction with the restrictiveness of identification guidelines. The research on identification and the contributions of leaders in the field such as Bloom (1985), Gardner (1983), Guilford (1977), Sternberg (1985), Torrance (1979), and Treffinger (1982) clearly point to the need to reexamine the regulations under which most programs are forced to operate and to develop more flexible approach to identification.

Schools should make every effort to develop reimbursement formulas that are based on total district enrollment rather than the number of students identified. It has been this "body count" approach that has forced schools to treat giftedness as an absolute state of being rather than a developmental concept; the result has been the most rigid kinds of test score identification procedures. Getting rid of the body count approach to identification allows districts greater flexibility in the types of identification and programming models they might want to consider (including test-based approaches) and provides greater equity for districts that serve disadvantaged and culturally diverse populations.

To be sure, a more broad approach to identification will result in a process that is a little less tidy, but the trade off for tidiness and administrative expediency will result in many more flexible approaches to both identification and programming. And with this flexibility will come new models for identifying and serving young people with great potential.

REFERENCES

Bloom, B. (Ed.) (1985*). Developing talent in young people.* New York: Ballantine.

Gardner, H. (1983). *Frames of mind* New York: Basic Books.

Guilford, J. P. (1977). *Way beyond the IQ.* Buffalo, NY: Bearly Limited.

Renzulli, J. S. (1977). *The enrichment triad model: A guide for developing defensible programs for the gifted and talented.* Mansfield Center, CT: Creative Learning Press.

Renzulli, J. S. (1986). The three-ring conception of giftedness: A developmental model for creative productivity. In Sternberg, R. J., & Davidson, J. (Eds.) *Conceptions of giftedness* (pp. 53-92). New York: Cambridge University Press.

Renzulli, J. S. (Ed.). (1988). *Technical report of research studies related to the enrichment triad/ revolving door model* (Third Edition). Teaching the Talented Program, University of Connecticut.

Renzulli, J. S., & Reis, S. M. (1997). *The schoolwide enrichment model: A comprehensive plan for educational excellence.* Mansfield Center, CT: Creative Learning Press.

Sternberg, R. (1985). A componential theory of intellectual giftedness. *Gifted Child Quarterly, 25,* 86-93.

Torrance, E. P. (1979). *The search for satori and creativity.* Buffalo, NY: Bearly Limited.

Treffinger, D. J. (1982). Demythologizing gifted education: An editorial essay. *Gifted Child Quarterly, 26*(1) 3-8.